Heartlifting
Blessings to

_____

May the eyes of your heart be enlightened so you will experience the eternal hope to which God has called you and the riches of His glorious inheritance for you. May your heart soar on the wings of His incredible, unfailing love.

God Loves You,

_____

_____

date

Ephesians 1:18

Surprising Stories, Stirring Messages, and Refreshing Scriptures That Make the Heart Soar

heartlifters™

for *Women*

LeAnn Weiss

messages by
Susan Duke

HOWARD
PUBLISHING CO.

Our purpose at Howard Publishing is to:

- *Increase faith* in the hearts of growing Christians
- *Inspire holiness* in the lives of believers
- *Instill hope* in the hearts of struggling people everywhere

Because He's coming again!

Heartlifters™ for Women © 1999 by LeAnn Weiss
All rights reserved. Printed in Hong Kong
Published by Howard Publishing Co., Inc., 3117 North 7th Street, West Monroe, Louisiana 71291-2227

00 01 02 03 04 05 06 07 08   10 9 8 7 6 5 4 3

Library of Congress Cataloging-in-Publication Data
　　Heartlifters for women : surprising stories, stirring messages,
and refreshing scriptures that make the heart soar / LeAnn Weiss ;
messages by Susan Duke.
　　　　p.　cm.
　　ISBN 1-58229-073-3
　　1. Christian women—Religious life.　I. Duke, Susan.　II. Title.
BV4527.W435　1999
242'.643—dc21　　　　　　　　　　99-30354
　　　　　　　　　　　　　　　　CIP

Personalized scriptures by LeAnn Weiss, owner of Encouragement Company
3006 Brandywine Dr., Orlando, FL 32806; (407) 898-4410

Edited by Philis Boultinghouse
Cover and interior design by LinDee Loveland
Photography by Lamar, Chrys Howard, and LinDee Loveland

Select photos courtesy of Biedenharn Museum and Gardens, Monroe, Louisiana

Contents

Commitment 1

Priorities 9

Giving 17

Honor 25

Simplicity 33

Confidence 41

Faith 49

When we are committed to

following, Christ will take us to

places we have never been before

and will teach us to see people as

we have never seen them before.

—JOSEPH M. STOWELL

Commitment

Even as a young child, her heart belonged wholly to God. She often prayed that He would allow her to die in His service.

She was born in China – delivered by her own father – during a chaotic period in that country's history. Her childhood heroes were Christian missionaries and Chinese converts, some of whom were murdered and many of whom were persecuted for their faith. Her father was a missionary-doctor who believed that his hospital existed "primarily for the preaching of the gospel." His love for the lost obviously beat in her heart as well. Stories of the 1900 Boxer Rebellion and accounts of church burnings and murders were common conversation – all of which molded and shaped her heart for her future life.

As she grew, her commitment to the Lord grew with her, and at the age of twelve, her dream was to become an "old maid missionary," serving God in the Himalayan Mountains of Tibet. When as a young woman she left China to attend college in the United States, she journaled, "If I marry…love must be so deep that it takes its stand in Christ and so wide that it takes the whole lost world in."

While in the United States, she found just such a love. Of the farm boy she married, she wrote, "He is a man of purpose, and that one purpose controls his whole heart and life." Her husband's single-hearted purpose took him away from home on many occasions, but because her heart was joined with his, she joyfully submitted to her role. Even before their marriage, she foreshadowed their future when she wrote, "After the joy and satisfaction of knowing that I am his by rights – and his forever – I will slip into the background."

Not long after their brief honeymoon, she developed a sore throat and fever. But her husband already had an out-of-town commitment, so he checked her into a hospital so she would receive the care she needed in his absence. She was discharged while he was gone, and when he returned home, he found that she had already settled into and tidied their new apartment.

Her busy husband missed the birth of their first child, and although he was there for the births of their other four children, she often felt like a single parent. Many tearful good-byes were exchanged at train stations and airports, as his work kept him away from home an average of six months a year. Because of the public nature of her husband's work, she and her children were forever under the glare of public scrutiny.

God's Word was her constant source of instruction, and His grace filled her with strength. She was truly the woman behind the man, and her letters, phone calls, prayers, counsel, encouragement, and research bolstered her husband and were vital to his success.

Writing in his autobiography, her husband praised, "The secret of Ruth's survival was in her commitment – not only her marriage commitment before God of her love for me, but also her ministry commitment of the two of us to the Lord's purpose for our lives together." Ruth Bell Graham, wife of beloved evangelist Billy Graham, challenges us all: "Let us accept each day as the Lord sends it, living obediently and faithfully, not fearing what may come, knowing that the glory ahead will obliterate the grim past, and praying we may be able to say to our Lord, 'We are honored to have served...under difficult circumstances.'"

In the good old days of yesteryear, your word was as good as a signed contract. And even contracts were often scribbled on torn portions of paper sacks. But these days, the very word commitment evokes a sense of challenge and fear.

Except to a child of God.

When you first felt God tugging at your heartstrings, you knew one thing: Inviting Him into your heart required commitment. But you were ready and willing to sign the promissory note, giving God sole ownership of your life. In return, He made a promise to you: He promised that if you would abide in Him, He would abide in you. He also promised that if you committed your life to Him, He would give you the desires of your heart.

Have you ever thought of commitment as a privilege? Throughout the Bible, we meet godly women of wisdom and strength who gave their lives in service to God. And the common thread of their deep inner characters? Commitment.

They committed their lives to serving others daily.

Your commitment allows God to demonstrate His abiding love through you. Laying aside your own agenda to fill a need in someone's life is commitment come alive. When you read a bedtime story to your children or help them with their homework, your commitment takes on a face. When you bake ten dozen cookies for PTA, when you iron your husband's shirt or pack an encouraging note in his lunch, when you help clean a friend's house for unexpected company or simply listen when her heart is broken, you've lived out your

commitment – not only to those in need but to the Lord. That's why He said, "When you did it for one of these, you did it for me."

Life's greatest treasures and blessings are wrapped in commitment – marriage, parenting, friend-ship, and the gift of God's infinite love.

Your commitment to God and His to you are not bound by rules or duty but by a two-way contract that binds your spirit with His. And there's no need for a signed agreement, for it is a covenant of the heart. Besides…He's given you His word, and you've given Him yours.

Commit your all to Me…

Life is too short to

spend it on the

urgent while

important things

slide by unnoticed.

—HEATHER WHITESTONE

Priorities

Elizabeth was born in 1936 in Salisbury, North Carolina. Many of her childhood Sunday afternoons were spent in her grandmother's living room, eating cookies, sipping ice-cold lemonade, and listening to Mom Cathey tell Bible stories. "The gospel was as much a part of our lives as fried chicken and azaleas in the spring," she recalled.

Voted most likely to succeed in high school, Elizabeth envisioned herself becoming just like Mom Cathey – always giving God top billing in her life. She contemplated becoming a Christian education director, but after graduating from Harvard Law School in 1965, she embarked on a career of public service in an arena dominated by men. In her own words, she was "drawn like a magnet" to Washington, D.C.

Beginning with her first government job in 1967, she held a post in five presidential administrations from Lyndon B. Johnson to George Bush. She married at age thirty-nine in 1975. She entered record books as one of the first female appointees in the Reagan administration, serving as assistant to the president for public liaison from 1981 to 1983.

But by 1982, a soul-searching Elizabeth realized that her escalating career was overshadowing the more important things of life. "Sunday had just become another day" – far from her goal of being like Mom Cathey.

"I had God neatly compartmentalized, crammed into a crowded file drawer of my life," she confessed in her 1988 National Prayer Breakfast address. "For if Christ is who He says He is – our Savior, the central figure in all of history, who gives meaning to a world of confusing, conflicting priorities – then I had to realize that Christ could not be compartmentalized. It was time to submit my resignation as master of my own universe, and God accepted my resignation."

By 1983, a more spiritually balanced Elizabeth set another historical record with her 1983 confirmation as Secretary of Transportation – becoming Ronald Reagan's first female cabinet member.

Then in 1989, she became George Bush's first female cabinet member, serving as Secretary of Labor. Her record-setting positions continued in 1991 when she became the first female president of the American Red Cross since founder Clara Barton. On her first day at the helm of the American Red Cross, Elizabeth shocked the world by announcing that she would turn down her $200,000 annual salary for the first year as a show of solidarity with the organization's volunteers.

Many are speculating that Elizabeth, named among the world's top three most admired women by a 1998 Gallup Poll, will become the first viable female U.S. presidential candidate. Despite her impressive résumé of "firsts," Elizabeth's priorities remain in focus. Life, according to Elizabeth Hanford Dole, is "a privilege, a responsibility, a stewardship to be lived according to a much higher calling – God's calling."

$\mathcal{D}$o you have days like I do when you're ready to hang a "Martha Stewart Doesn't Live Here" sign in your window? Does the struggle to simplify your life seem to get more complicated by the hour? Endless to-do lists of carpooling, laundry, dishes, grocery shopping, committee meetings, business deadlines, errands, and cooking can leave you feeling drained and overwhelmed. And then there's the time you need to set aside for your husband and friends and the hours you need to schedule for your projects and goals. It can all seem like too much! But remember that Martha Stewart employs help! And even the Proverbs 31 woman's accomplishments were not all done in a day. (Try a lifetime!)

The key to balance is not found in making better lists or putting unrealistic demands on yourself to become Superwoman.

The key is found in putting God first, fine-tuning your heart to His, and taking time to sit at His feet and listen as He directs your steps. Finding all of yourself in Him rather than merely finding a place for Him in yourself changes the desires of your heart and your devotion.

God has armed you with all the power you'll ever need to be the woman He's created you to be. But that power is derived more from inspiration than aspiration. Spending time with God is not a blessing we give to Him; it is a blessing He gives to us.

So relax, put your feet up, pour yourself a cup of tea, close your eyes, and invite Him into the living room of your heart. Just think, the Creator of the Universe is eager to spend time alone with you – just you and Him.

He's ready to listen, and He's eager to offer encouragement, direction, and refreshment for your soul.

In the stillness He may whisper, "Don't feel guilty. I never intended for you to say yes to everyone and everything that comes along. More than all of your doing, learning the art of 'being' pleases Me and better serves others. Besides, I've created all the time you'll ever need."

Put Me first, always…

It's not how much we give

but how much love

we put into giving.

—MOTHER TERESA

Giving

Following in the footsteps of her mother and grandmother, Oseola began washing and ironing laundry after school when she was only eight years old. The dollar-fifty to two dollars that she earned per bundle was used to help support her family. Oseola's dream of becoming a nurse evaporated when she had to drop out of sixth grade to care for an ailing aunt. By the time her aunt recovered, Oseola was too far behind in her studies to continue her education.

As a young woman, Oseola developed the habit of living frugally and saving her money. Gleaning wisdom from her Bible, she learned to be content in her simple life. When her fee for a load of laundry grew to ten dollars, she regularly deposited most of her earnings into a savings account and

bought only the barest necessities for herself. Oseola never married, and following the deaths of her mother and aunt in the sixties, she was left alone. She lived in a meager wood-framed house without air conditioning, even during the hot Mississippi summers. A basic black-and-white TV, her dog, and a pig were Oseola's only companions. She never owned a car, and whenever she needed to buy groceries, she pushed a shopping cart one mile to and from the store.

For more than seventy-five years, Oseola quietly toiled, working six days a week, sometimes ironing until three o'clock in the morning. In 1994, at age eighty-six, gnarling arthritis forced her to retire from her scrubboard. No one but her local Hattiesburg, Mississippi, banker suspected how much Oseola's accumulated nest egg was now worth.

In July of 1995, Oseola signed an irrevocable trust bequeathing 60 percent of her life's savings to a scholarship for needy African-Americans at the University of Southern Mississippi. It never occurred to her that she was doing anything remarkable. Officials at USM were amazed at the 150,000 dollar gift from a washerwoman who had never even visited their school, but no one expected the national media frenzy that followed. Soon, Oseola's self-less deed was spotlighted by top TV networks, David Letterman, the *New York Times*, *People*, *Life*, *Newsweek*, and numerous publications worldwide.

Oseola's generosity boomeranged, and she herself became the recipient of the generosity of others. She was instantly plucked from a life of obscurity and eventually honored with more than sixty-two awards. Her first trip outside the South was to the White House, where President Clinton praised her "remarkable example of spirit and ingenuity that made America great." Harvard University presented her with an honorary doctorate, and USM esteemed her with its first ever honorary degree. In 1996, she was chosen to carry the Olympic torch. On New Year's Eve 1997, in New York's Time Square, an enthusiastic crowd of more than 500,000 people cheered as Oseola flipped the switch that lowered the famous New Year's Eve ball.

Since setting up the Oseola McCarty Scholarship Fund, Oseola has had the opportunity to share with audiences around the country encouraging young people to stay in school. Her spirit of giving has also inspired others to contribute to the scholarship fund. To date, more than 450,000 dollars of additional money for the fund has poured in from thirty states and more than six hundred individuals, businesses, and corporations. Regarding her initial seed money, Oseola McCarty regrets, "I only wish I had more to give."

Your heart is like a garden. God has planted seeds in its fertile ground and given you an abundant harvest so that you might bless others. The Master Gardner carefully designed these special seeds to reproduce again and again, and when God's love takes root in your heart, a fervent desire to give begins to bloom. From one harvest of giving to the next, an endless bounty of loving generosity flourishes in your heart.

And what you give to others reproduces again and again. You may never know how your giving fills a heart with new hope, waters a dormant seed of kindness that springs to life, or brings in a long-awaited harvest of joy.

God's Word says to give as you have purposed in your heart (see 2 Corinthians 9:7). Has compassion for a sick friend been planted in your heart's garden? Then, from compassion's harvest, purpose to offer a pot of soup or an encouraging visit. Has the desire to show appreciation to a special someone bloomed in your heart? Then send a card, a hand-written note, or a care package filled with goodies. When you do these things, you give with purpose from a heart cultivated by God Himself. When you give money, time, and talents, you give eternal gifts from the heart...gifts that keep on giving.

Biedenharn Museum and Gardens

You've heard the saying "It's the thought that counts." How true! Perhaps "thought" is the name of the seed that God first plants in our giving garden. It's the thought that produces the needed gift and accomplishes love's true purpose.

Aren't you glad that when God thought of you, He purposely gave heaven's most treasured gift – Jesus? Allow the bounty of His love to bloom in your heart until a garden of generosity flourishes and produces heavenly fruit.

Give to others out of My bounty…

photography by Lamar

The Lord is the source of honor, the One

from whom it flows.... We have the power

to treat others as valuable treasures

because He treats us that way.

—GARY SMALLEY AND JOHN TRENT

Honor

At age six, a seed was planted in the heart of Flo when she nursed her first patient, an injured collie dog, back to health. By age seventeen, she wrote, "God called me to His service" – nursing.

But in the early 1800s, nursing was an undesirable occupation, typically left to prostitutes, alcoholics, and other down-and-out people. Her wealthy, aristocratic parents vehemently opposed her plans to become a nurse, thinking she would be wasting her destiny of privilege. Torn between her parents' wishes and her own, on her thirtieth birthday, Flo journaled, "Lord, let me think only of Thy Will." In 1851 she followed what she believed to be the will of God, and

shunning her social status, she donned the muslin cap and blue cotton dress of nurses in training.

One fall morning in 1854, Flo read an article in the *Times* that changed her life. Regarding the barbarously inhumane conditions of the Crimean War and the need for help, the empassioned journalist wrote, "Are none of the daughters of England, at this extreme hour of need, ready for such a work of mercy?" Flo cried when she learned that because there were so few doctors and absolutely no nurses, British soldiers were dying without even the most basic care. Her response was quick and sure: "Here am I, Lord, send me."

Now a successful nursing superintendent, Flo left the comforts of home to lead a team of nurses to Turkey. Within hours of her arrival, five hundred wounded soldiers were added to the thousand-plus patients that were already under her direct responsibility.

Filthy hygiene, infectious disease, rats, and food shortages confronted her at every turn. But even with the horrific conditions and the long, arduous work hours — sometimes twenty-four hours straight — her compassion for the suffering never lagged. Her social status afforded by her heritage connected her with politically powerful individuals whom she hounded for support of her cause. Writing more than twelve thousand letters and hundreds of reports over the course of her career, she aroused England's conscience, and through her efforts substantial money and supplies were furnished to her sick and dying soldiers.

Each midnight hour Flo could be seen carrying her lantern, tirelessly walking the four-mile rows of beds, checking every single soldier. It was Longfellow who immortalized her in his poem as the "lady with the lamp."

By the close of the war, with 125 well-trained nurses under her supervision, the mortality rate had sharply declined. After the war, her reform efforts focused on improving health and sanitation conditions back home.

In 1855, Queen Victoria honored Flo with a brooch inscribed "Blessed are the merciful." Saluting her "pure spirit of duty toward God and compassion for man," Lord Stanley characterized her as one of the top two people to impact English history within the past one hundred years.

In 1859, Flo's *Notes on Nursing* became an international bestseller. Her training programs and models for hospitals established Flo, better known as Florence Nightingale, as the Mother of Modern Nursing.

$\mathcal{D}$oesn't it feel good to know that you've done something to the very best of your ability? I'm not talking about pride but about the gentle satisfaction that warms your heart when you know that your contribution has made a difference — when you've given "honorably, as unto the Lord," the gifts and talents that are uniquely yours.

No one else can do what you can do. Some people spend a lifetime trying to develop a gift rather than looking within the treasure chests of their hearts to find what is already there.

What motivates you? What do you feel passionately about? Do you love organizing? Are you

Biedenharn Museum and Gardens

good at teaching or speaking? Do
people love to hear your stories? Are
you driven to find solutions when a
need arises? Are you the first to make
soup or care for someone who is sick?

When you open your heart to
using the gifts God has already placed
within you, opportunities to use those
gifts will spring up before you. Your
willingness to exercise your God-given
talents will open doors to places you
never dreamed of. There's a peace
that comes from being in the center of
God's will and knowing that what you
do brings honor to Him.

A job well done may incidentally put you in the spotlight and bring honor and recognition to you, just as Christ's gift of healing brought him attention and praise. But Jesus was quick to point to the Father and give Him all the glory. This must be your response as well. Exercising your gift honorably is sacred, holy, a form of worship, and a noble tribute to the Gift Giver.

You are God's handmaiden. What you are is God's gift to you. What you become is your gift back to God. May you shine as a beacon of light for His glory!

I will make your righteousness shine like the dawn…

The hunger in our hearts for a saner, simpler place is part of the evidence that

such a place exists. God has put this hunger in us to draw us to

himself, his way, his kingdom, his Son.

—CLAIRE CLONINGER

Simplicity

Bessie was in her late twenties when her first published story – a letter to the editor describing her family's trek across the frontier in their move to Missouri – appeared in her hometown paper. But farm life afforded little time for writing, and Bessie turned her energy to matters of the barn-yard, eventually becoming a recognized chicken expert. On one occassion, she was invited to speak to a farm group but was unable to attend, so she wrote out her speech and had it read to the group. Sitting in the audience was editor of the *Missouri Ruralist*. He was impressed enough with her writing that he contacted her and suggested she submit articles for his bimonthly farm paper.

Her writing focus broadened as time went by, and she

began to write of simple beauties and observations from everyday life. Bessie once reflected in her column, "I am beginning to learn that it is the sweet, simple things of life which are the real ones after all."

Her first national exposure came when her daughter, Rose, an accomplished writer, helped her get "Whom Will You Marry?" – an article about marriage from a farm woman's perspective – published in *McCall's* magazine. Other articles, "My Ozark Kitchen" and "The Farm Dining Room," were published in *Country Gentleman*. When Bessie's mother died, Bessie's heart was stirred to collect and preserve stories of her own childhood.

Rose edited her mother's childhood memoirs and submitted them to several national magazines. They all declined to publish them, but the *Saturday Evening Post* editor saw potential in Bessie's writing and encouraged her to rewrite the stories in a fictional format.

Bessie's daughter also submitted Bessie's stories to be used as the storyline for a children's picture book. After a positive response from the juvenile department of Alfred A. Knopf, Bessie expanded one of her stories into a novel for eight-to-twelve-year-old readers, adding details of everyday life. But sadly, Knopf's children's division closed during the Depression before the book could be published. Instead, Bessie received word on Thanksgiving Day that Harper and Row would publish her children's book. Published when Bessie was sixty-five, *Little House in the Big Woods* was an instantaneous bestseller. Her next seven novels, also fictionalized stories based on her life, became popular children's classics.

Enthusiasm about her books was reborn with the airing of the popular television series inspired by her stories: *Little House on the Prairie*. Melissa Gilbert played the role of "Bessie," known to the public as Laura.

Laura's novels – written between 1932 and 1943 – continue to delight children around the world and provide us all with a historically accurate glimpse of daily American frontier life. Laura, the pioneer girl, wrote about journeying across the country in a covered wagon, singing hymns as "Pa" played the fiddle, blizzards, Indian raids, grasshoppers, prairie fires, sickness, and death. Cherished scriptures were referenced in the margins of her worn Bible: "In facing a crisis; read 48 Psalm." "When discouraged; Psalm 23 & 24."

In 1947, Laura wrote to schoolchildren: "The way we live and your schools are much different now…but the real things haven't changed. It is still best to be honest and truthful; to make the most of what we have; to be happy with simple pleasures and to be cheerful." In 1957, Laura Ingalls Wilder took her first airplane ride just shortly before her death at ninety years of age.

$\mathcal{D}$o you long for a less complicated, less frantic way of living? Do you yearn for the simple life of days gone by? You're not alone. For the past few years, there's been a renewed interest in the peace of "simplicity." Bookstore shelves are filled with books on how to simplify your life. People everywhere seek relief from their chaotic, stressful lives.

But finding simplicity requires more than tossing the clutter out of your closet. It demands rearranging your lifestyle. Too often we strive, push, and race ahead like a run-away train barreling down rick-ety tracks to destinations labeled "success." But God has provided a different kind of path, if we will choose it. This path leads to spiritual refreshment, godly maturity, and peace of mind.

Simplicity is that place that speaks, through the ashes of shattered dreams and grown-up ambition, to the child inside who's longing to embrace life — yearning to savor its abundance. It's the voice that invites you to live moment by moment, not plan by plan. With welcoming embrace, it dispels the clutter of agendas and sets a table of joy, hope, love, and simple pleasures.

Simplicity will not be dropped in your lap — you must pursue it. But its realization is only a prayer away. Right now, lay aside cluttered thoughts and take a spiritual journey inward. Think about some of your favorite things: Do you love curling up in an old quilt by a crackling fire? Have you ever marveled at the colors of a crimson sunset or walked barefoot along a warm, sandy beach? Perhaps

Biedenharn Museum and Gardens

the smell of a fresh apple pie baking in the oven or the feel of gentle, soft snowflakes falling on your face is what warms your heart. Think of a song you love, your favorite season, or sweet remembrances of friends and loved ones who fill your life with joy. Simple pleasures — soul-nourishing indulgences of endearment — are only a heartbeat away.

When we're still enough to listen, we'll hear an ever-beckoning cry calling our hearts home to simplicity, a path only the heart can follow.

Come to Me for rest…

photography by Lamar

My own self-confidence is tied up in the character of God,

so I don't have to worry about it.

—MARY C. CROWLEY

Confidence

As a child, Hadassah was adopted and raised by her cousin when death claimed the lives of both natural parents. She and her cousin lived as exiles in Susa, the capital city of a pagan empire extending from Ethiopia to India.

Hadassah grew into a beautiful young woman, and when the king of the land instituted a search for a new queen, Hadassah was one of the many young virgins chosen for review. Heeding her cousin's stern instructions, Hadassah told no one of her heritage.

When Hadassah met privately with the king, her inner as well as outer beauty gripped his lonely heart. To him, there was no contest – she was his favorite.

After several years, life's royal trappings became standard

for Queen Hadassah. Her life, once obscure, was now marked with royalty and nobility. But one day, her past resurfaced when a powerful man in the kingdom began plotting a full-scale ethnic cleansing, targeting all men, women, and children of her secret ancestry.

Hadassah had a choice to make. The cousin who had strictly forbidden her from revealing her family background now entreated her to go before the king, reveal her true identity, and beg for mercy for her people.

But Hadassah was afraid. Everyone knew that anyone who approached the king without being summoned faced imminent death. Besides, the plan for the holocaust of her people had already been published and publicly confirmed. And once a king's edict had been issued, it was irreversible. What could she – one woman – do?

But her cousin's challenge hit its mark: "Do you think that because you are in the king's house that you alone will escape? And who knows but that you have come to royal position for such a time as this?"

Hadassah called upon her people to fast and pray for three days and confidently announced that she would go before the king at the end of the three days, even with the looming possibility of death.

When Hadassah approached the King unsummoned, he immediately extended his golden scepter as a sign of favor for his beloved queen. Although the edict could not be revoked, the king granted Hadassah's people the right to defend themselves against the coming attack. Hadassah's people won an overwhelming victory over their assailants. The brave actions of this once obscure minority orphan and her cousin averted the planned annihilation of her entire race throughout the kingdom.

Today, Jewish people around the world celebrate Purim on the fourteenth and fifteenth days of the month of Adar in commemoration of the deliverance of the Jews by Queen Hadassah and her cousin Mordecai. Queen Hadassah's life is documented in the Old Testament of the Bible in the book named after her more commonly known Persian name, Esther. Esther means "star," and like her name, Queen Esther confidently shined during her arduous challenge, knowing that she had come to her royal position for such a time as this.

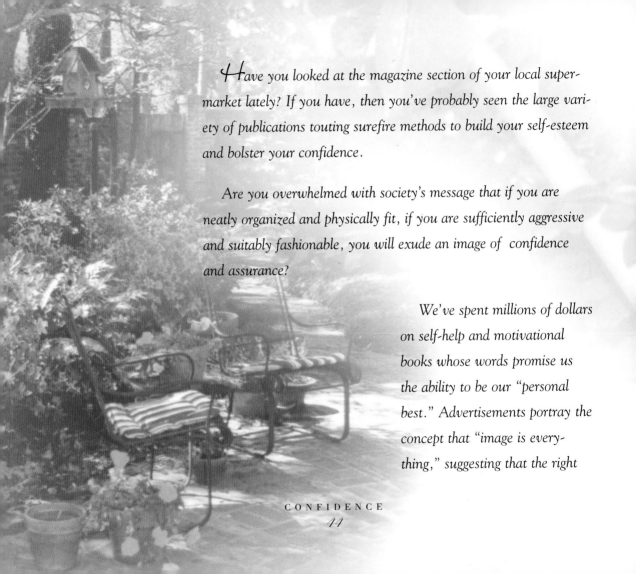

Have you looked at the magazine section of your local supermarket lately? If you have, then you've probably seen the large variety of publications touting surefire methods to build your self-esteem and bolster your confidence.

Are you overwhelmed with society's message that if you are neatly organized and physically fit, if you are sufficiently aggressive and suitably fashionable, you will exude an image of confidence and assurance?

We've spent millions of dollars on self-help and motivational books whose words promise us the ability to be our "personal best." Advertisements portray the concept that "image is everything," suggesting that the right kind of cereal, shampoo, coffee, or toothpaste will change your life. Even Uncle Sam tells you to "be all you can be...in the army."

You were born in search of significance. But when you accepted God's love, your search ended. God says you are a woman of worth – fearfully and wonderfully made – just as you are, right now! His Word also declares self-confidence as false security. Our confidence is in Him, not in ourselves. When we rely on and trust Him completely, He promises to be our shield.

It's great to live a healthy lifestyle, take personal time-outs, and aspire to accomplish goals. But the Bible warns that when we have confidence in our own strength, beauty, or righteousness, we are in reality fools. When your motives for excellence stem from a heart sold out to God, you achieve true confidence – not from your own abilities but from an inward peace based on God's righteous work in you.

You are a valuable, precious representative of the One who created you. You have a crucial role in God's kingdom. You are a child of the Most High God, the King's kid. You are the salt of the earth and the apple of His eye. Within you is His "personal best." Your earthen vessel holds the excellency of power – God (see 2 Corinthians 4:7).

Knowing who you are in Christ and who He is in you gives you all the confidence you'll ever need to "be all that you can be" in His army.

You are My masterpiece…

Faith sings in your heart, no matter

what assaults your soul.

—LESTER SUMRALL

Faith

Wedding plans were delayed when Nabby's husband-to-be was inoculated and quarantined during a highly contagious smallpox epidemic. But Nabby's devotion was steadfast, and she faithfully wrote her fiancé, John, every day of their five-week separation. John was a Harvard law school graduate, while Nabby had no formal education. Yet she was one of the most well-read females of her time.

Nabby's first year of marriage was marked by the birth of their first child and by the British government's enactment of the infamous Stamp Tax, which her husband strongly opposed. As a successful attorney, her husband traveled the court circuit, frequently leaving Nabby alone in their Braintree, Massachusetts, home.

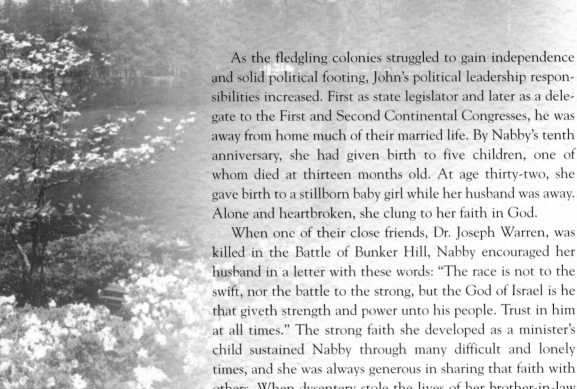

As the fledgling colonies struggled to gain independence and solid political footing, John's political leadership responsibilities increased. First as state legislator and later as a delegate to the First and Second Continental Congresses, he was away from home much of their married life. By Nabby's tenth anniversary, she had given birth to five children, one of whom died at thirteen months old. At age thirty-two, she gave birth to a stillborn baby girl while her husband was away. Alone and heartbroken, she clung to her faith in God.

When one of their close friends, Dr. Joseph Warren, was killed in the Battle of Bunker Hill, Nabby encouraged her husband in a letter with these words: "The race is not to the swift, nor the battle to the strong, but the God of Israel is he that giveth strength and power unto his people. Trust in him at all times." The strong faith she developed as a minister's child sustained Nabby through many difficult and lonely times, and she was always generous in sharing that faith with others. When dysentery stole the lives of her brother-in-law and mother and severely threatened the life of her son Tommy, she affirmed: "Yea though he slay me I will trust in him.... What though his corrective Hand hath been stretched against me; I will not murmur. Though earthly comforts are taken away I will not pine."

Nabby was again left alone with her children when John was chosen to serve on the committee to draft the Declaration of Independence. While he was gone, two of their children became critically ill with smallpox.

In February of 1778, she said another sad farewell to both her husband and oldest son when they sailed to France to gain French assistance against England, leaving Nabby and the rest of her children alone once again. During the six-and-a-half-year separation, she lamented, "Religion, thy force can alone support the Mind under the severest trials and hardest conflicts humane Nature is subject to." After only a short four-month reunion, her husband was summoned back to France to negotiate terms for the Treaty of Paris, officially ending the war.

Over the years, Nabby wrote more than two thousand letters – to her husband, her sisters, and her friends – documenting her faith as well as the political characters and historical events that shaped the Revolutionary War and the bedrock years of America. She once reflected, "My heart is made soft by many afflictions."

Nabby, formally known as Abigail Smith Adams, was the first, first lady to live in the White House after the U.S. capital was changed to Washington, D.C., during her husband's, John Adams, term as the second president of the United States. Wife to the second U.S. president, she was also mother to the sixth – John Quincy Adams. The entirety of Abigail's influence on our country will never be known.

We all have "Red Sea" moments in our lives. You know, those situations when we're certain that unless God moves on our behalf, we'll drown. But so often we stand on the precipice, facing our "Red Sea," wearing a "just in case" inner tube – proclaiming all the while that we have faith.

Living faith looks impossibility in the face and sings a song of victory before the battle is won, and faith's expression is frequently in the voice of praise. It's easy to praise Him after we've reached the other side. But praising God before He parts the sea, before the answer comes, before we are delivered from adversity displays our undaunted trust in Him and Him alone. Faith with feet trusts God to part the waters just in time to walk across dry land to His promise.

Children are great teachers, especially in the faith department, and Jesus said we should pattern our faith after theirs. Children believe without reservation or hesitation. Have you ever observed a child just before he jumped from a diving board – his eyes focused on the waiting arms of his father or mother? God, our Father, longs to see the same kind of childlike faith in you and me, a faith that leaps fearlessly into His waiting, outstretched arms.

Childhood faith is no better exemplified than in the little boy who

gave his meager offering of loaves and fish to Jesus on the mountainside. He believed that when given to Jesus, it would somehow be enough. It was. That's why Jesus says that if we only have a little faith – even the size of a mustard seed – we can speak to mountains and they'll be removed!

True faith is coming to the edge of a cliff in the darkness and believing God will catch you or teach you to fly. As one choir anthem declares, "Faith is stepping out on nothing and landing on something."

Faith means we can thank God in advance for His answer.

Be sure of
what you hope for…

photography by Lamar

God will never let you be shaken or moved from your place near His heart.

—JONI EARECKSON TADA

Write your own story of how God has shaped your life and used you for His purpose.

_____

_____

_____

_____

_____

_____

_____

_____

_____

Other books that include
LeAnn Weiss's paraphrased Scriptures

Hugs for Dad
Hugs for Grandparents
Hugs for the Holidays
Hugs for the Hurting
Hugs for Mom
Hugs for Women
Hugs to Encourage and Inspire
Hugs from Heaven: Embraced by the Savior
Hugs from Heaven: On Angel Wings

Also by LeAnn Weiss

Hugs for Friends
Heartlifters™ *for Hope and Joy*

Sources

Over one hundred sources were used in compiling the biographical sketches in this book. The following sources were primary.

Ruth Bell Graham

Cornwell, Patricia. *Ruth, A Portrait: The Story of Ruth Bell Graham*. New York: Doubleday, 1997.

Graham, Billy. *Just As I Am: The Autobiography of Billy Graham*. New York: HarperCollins Publishers, 1997.

Elizabeth Dole

Woodbridge, John, ed. *Portraits of Believers from All Walks of Life*. Chicago: Moody Press, 1992.

Ferranti, Jennifer. "A Godly Heritage: Elizabeth Dole's Success Traces to Her Spiritual Upbringing." *Power for Living* (Colorado Springs: SP Publications) 57, no. 1 (1998).

Oseola McCarty

Special thanks to the University of Southern Mississippi Public Relations, Oseola McCarty Scholarship Fund, USM Foundation, Box 10026, Hattiesburg, Miss. 39406.

McCarty, Oseola. *Oseola McCarty's Simple Wisdom for Rich Living*. Atlanta: Longstreet Press, 1996.

Florence Nightingale

    Miller, Basil. *Florence Nightingale: The Lady of the Lamp*. Minneapolis, Minn.: Bethany House Publishers, 1975.

Laura Ingalls Wilder

    Hines, Stephen W. *I Remember Laura*. Nashville: Thomas Nelson Publishers, 1994.

    Miller, John E. *Becoming Laura Ingalls Wilder: The Woman behind the Legend*. Columbia, Mo.: University of Missouri Press, 1998.

Esther

    Swindoll, Charles R. *Esther: A Woman of Strength and Dignity*. Nashville: Word Publishing, 1997.

    The Holy Bible, New International Version. Grand Rapids, Mich.: Zondervan Publishing House, 1984.

Abigail Adams Smith

    Akers, Charles W. *Abigail Adams: An American Woman*. Boston: Little, Brown and Company, 1980.

    Whitley, Lynne. *Dearest Friend: A Life of Abigail Adams*. New York: The Free Press, 1981.